Delicious Japan by Month

Ari Idee

Delicious Japan by Month by Ari Idee

Copyright © 2013 Technology and Imagination Press
Text and Illustrations copyright © 2013 by Ari Idee
All rights reserved.

No part of this publication may be reproduced, stored in a retrieval system, or transmitted
in any form or by any means, electronic, mechanical, photocopying, recording ,
or otherwise, without written permission of the publisher.
For information, on getting permission for reprints and excerpts,
contact tip_books@happyhippocreations.com

ISBN: 0-9798991-1-7
ISBN-13: 978-0-9798991-1-9

First Printing 2013

Delicious Japan by Month

Ari Idee

January

On New Year's Day, Japanese people welcome the God of Grains. They believe God visits houses that have the New Year's decorative pine tree branches, *Kadomatsu*. People offer God a round rice cake, *Kagami-mochi*. They eat special cuisine in boxes, *Osechi*. Every food symbolizes a different wish.

Osechi   *Kagami-mochi*

Prawn (*Ebi*): Longevity. Prawns have long whiskers and hunched back like an old man.

Rolled Omelet (*Date-Maki*): High education. It looks like a scroll.

Black Beans (*Kuro-Mame*): Health and fortune. The color black has the power to sweep evil away.

Mashed Sweet Potato with Sweetened Chestnuts (*Kinton*): Gold and treasure. It looks like the color of gold.

Herring Roe (*Kazunoko*): Numerous offspring.

Rolled Kelp (*Kobu-maki*): Good luck. *Kobu-maki* is part of *Yorokobu* which means "being happy" in Japanese.

Fish Cake (*Kamaboko*): The combination of red and white means good luck.

Red Sea Bream (*Tai*): Good luck. *Tai* is a part of *Medetai* which means "happy" in Japanese.

Setsubun Mame
(Roasted Soy Bean)

February

February Third is called *Setsubun*, the day for expelling ogres. People throughout Japan throw roast soy beans at a person who plays the ogre. This is a ceremony to expel evil. An old saying goes if people eat as many beans as their age, they will have good health for a year.

In Southern Japan, people eat vinegary rice rolled in dried seaweed. In ancient times, people believed if they ate it with their eyes closed and imagined their dreams, facing to a lucky direction, their dreams would come true. Today, modern people follow this practice from long custom.

Futo-maki (Rice rolled in dried seaweed)

March

March Third is the Dolls' Festival. Families with girls display a set of dolls to celebrate the health of their daughters. The practice of using sets of dolls began a long time ago, Japanese people threw human shaped paper dolls into rivers to cleanse real people of evil or bad luck. Hundreds of years later, in the Edo period (1603-1868), people started displaying the doll set used today in the Dolls' Festival. These dolls, wearing elaborately woven kimonos, portray an imperial wedding.

Adults enjoy drinking sweet white *Sake* during festivals.

Chirashi Sushi

Hishi mochi (Rice cake)

Hina-Arare (Rice cracker)

During the Dolls' Festival, Japanese people eat *Chirashi Sushi*, a kind of sushi which is in a wooden box with lots of ingredients on top. The main ingredients may include shrimp, shredded omelet, string bean, salmon sashimi, salmon roe, lotus root, and shiitake mushroom. This sushi conveys the wish of the parents that their girls will have abundant food even after they have left their home to be married.

Japanese people give the dolls diamond-shaped rice cakes (*hishi mochi*) and tiny rice crackers (*Hina-Arare*.)Both of them are colored pink, white, and green with extract of gardenia and Japanese mugwort. These three colors depict peach, snow, and fresh leaves.

The Dolls' Festival celebrates girls with food and ritual using figures that have been used in Japan for centuries. Its purpose is to assure a happy marriage for Japanese daughters. The festival still has great significance to the Japanese and the dolls are carefully treated and stored.

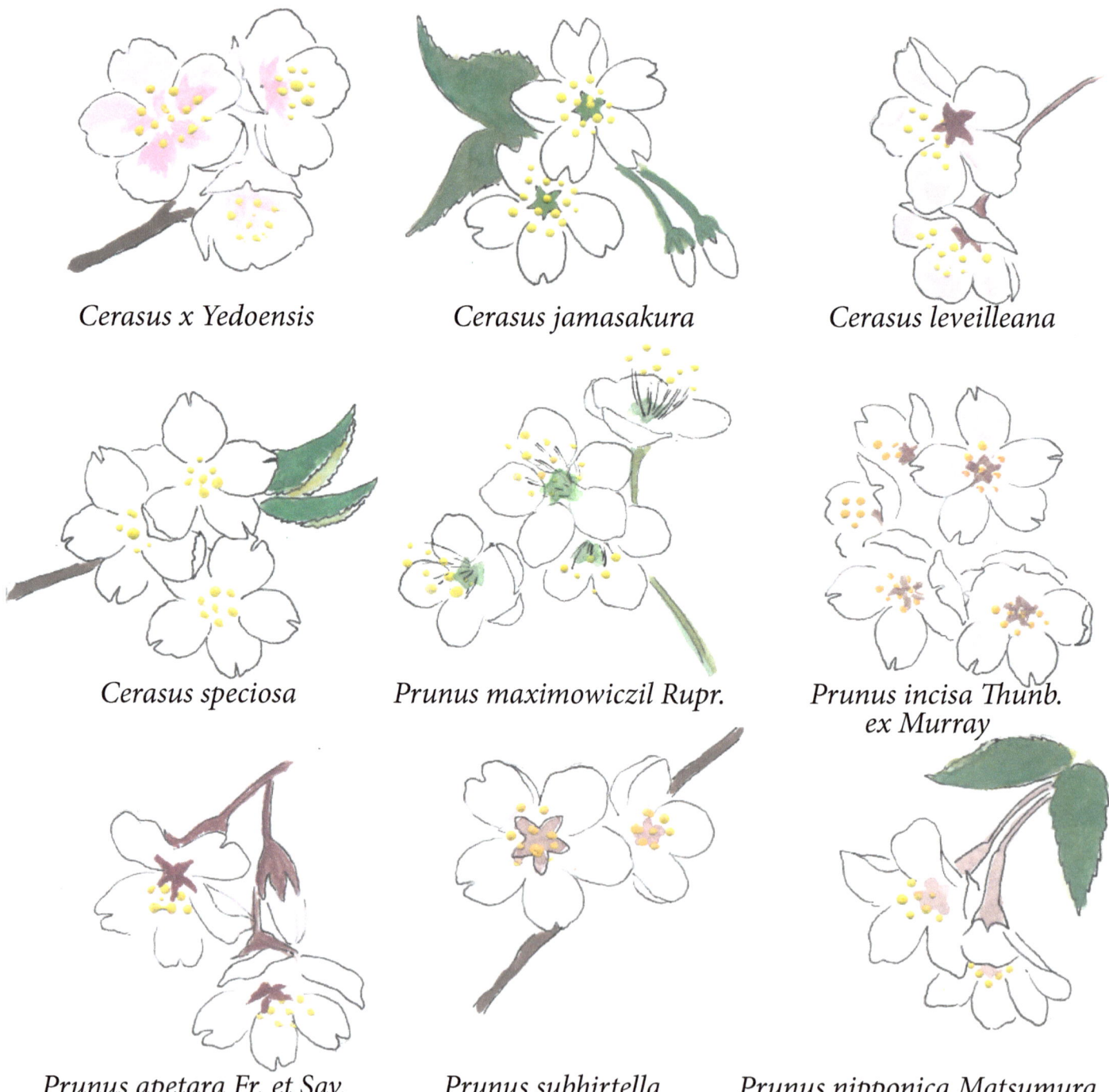

April

Japanese people enjoy viewing cherry blossoms in April. Celebrating the appearance of Cherry blossoms in April is a practice that began in Japan in the seventh century and has now spread throughout the world. The trees blossom at different times depending upon the area, trees, and condition of the weather.

In the seventh century, Japanese aristocrats started Cherry blossom viewing as a yearly ritual. They composed poems to praise the beauty of blossoms under the cherry trees. In the seventeenth century, cherry blossom viewing was spread to the common people. Today, people go out to parks, gardens, mountains, and riversides to enjoy viewing the cherry blossom while eating skewered sweet rice dumplings or boxed meal and drinking alcoholic beverages.

The Cherry blossom is the most special flower to the Japanese people. They love the way cherry blossoms bloom quickly and fall gracefully. There are nine kinds of wild cherry blossoms and over 600 manmade hybrids.

Hanami Dango (Sticky rice balls)

May

May Fifth is called "Kids' Day" which is part of a national holiday week starting April 29. During this many museums and other facilities for children are free. May Fifth is primarily a celebration for boys. Families with boys display carp shaped streamers outside and Japanese ancient warriors' helmets or armor at home.

The streamers are called *Koi-Nobori*. These carp streamers are attached to a pole which is about 16 feet. They convey the wish of the parents that their boys will succeed in life like carps that can swim in a torrent or go upstream in a waterfall. Warriors' helmets and armor are symbols of strength and life protection. Parents wish their boys to grow strong and healthy.

On May Fifth, Japanese people take a bath with iris leaves to drive evil away. Tradition also says if people wrap their heads with iris leaves, they will get smarter.

During this festival, Japanese people eat a special sweet called Kashiwa-Mochi. It is a sticky rice cake filled with sweet red bean paste. This sweet is wrapped with an oak leaf. Since oak trees don't shed their leaves until the young leaves come out, the oak trees symbolize long family lines with many descendants. "Kids Day" shows the importance of children to the Japanese people.

Kashiwa-Mochi
(Sticky rice cake filled with red bean paste)

June

The rainy season in the main land of Japan begins June and continues to mid-July. It is caused by the collision of cold northerly air and warm southerly air. This climate affects the southernmost prefecture, Okinawa, about a month earlier, and does not affect northernmost island, Hokkaido. During this season, most Japanese people suffer the dump air and mold.

Despite the humidity, they enjoy viewing hydrangeas and their changing colors. Many temples have Hydrangea Festivals throughout Japan. Before modern medical treatment became available, the rainy season caused many illness and death. "Hydrangea Temples" comforted the deceased. Today, blooming hydrangeas in those temples are a key element of sightseeing.

July

July Seventh is called *Tanabata*, the "Star Festival." This festival originated from a Chinese legend about two stars. Vega, a weaver, and Altair, a cow herder, were lovers who spent more time playing than working. Vega's father, the emperor, got upset and separated them by placing the Milky Way between them. However, he allowed them to meet each other once a year on July Seventh.

On this day, Japanese people decorate bamboo branches with oblong paper and other paper ornaments to celebrate the lovers' reunion. People believe their wishes will come true if they write them on the paper and hang them on branches.

On July Seventh, families eat very fine white noodles, called *So-Men*, that are nourishing enough to overcome the summer heat. *So-men* noodles also symbolizes the Milky Way and the thread Vega was weaving with. This is the day that even people who usually have no interests in the sky, tend to look up at it.

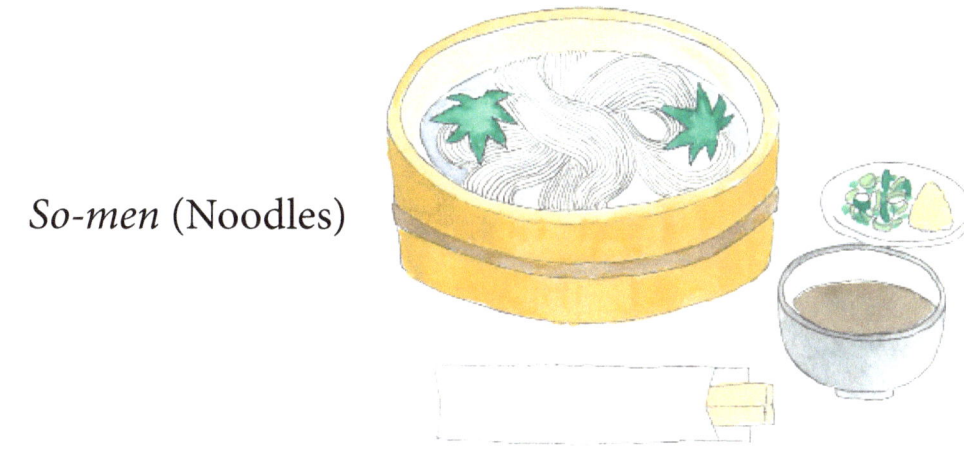

So-men (Noodles)

August

Around August 15th, most Japanese people take long holidays. They are called the *Bon* holidays and many people go back to their hometown to get together with their families and to visit their ancestors' graves. Japanese people believes spirits come back to their homes during this holidays.

Usually on August 16th, the *Bon* Festival is held in shrines, parks, or public spaces. Men and women of all ages wear kimonos and dance to music around and on a temporary wooden tower. This dance represents the joyful dance of the dead escaped from the ordeals in hell.

In the *Bon* Festival, many stands sell various kinds of food such as shaved ice, grilled chicken on skewers, and fried noodles. At home, people offer sticky rice balls coated by sweet red bean paste, sesame, or soy bean flower to their ancestors. They also eat these dishes themselves. When rice and sugar were valuable, making this sweet dish and offering it to deceased was considered to be accumulating a good deed. Since it is a series of long holidays, with the chance to meet family and old friends, most Japanese people look forward to the *Bon* Festivals.

Ohagi (Sticky rice balls coated with red bean paste)

September

Moon viewing is held on August 15th in the lunar calendar. Japanese people have been appreciating the full moon since the ninth century. The nobles got on a small boat and composed poems while looking at the reflection of the Moon. They did not look at the moon directly as they thought viewing the moon reflected in water or sake was more elegant than looking at the moon directly. Today, people display Japanese pampas grass and offer dumpling, taro, and sake while also enjoying this food and drink themselves. Unlike the ancients, modern people usually look at the moon directly.

Tsukimi Dango (Dumplings)

October

October is the month that many trees start putting on their autumn colors. In Hokkaido, however, the northernmost island, the leaves start changing color in September. Okinawa, the southernmost island, barely has autumn at all.

Japanese people enjoy viewing the red, orange, and yellow colors on maple trees in the mountains. They call the custom *Momiji-Gari*, "Maple Hunting." It started among the nobles in the Nara era (710-794) and Heian Era (794-1185) and was established as a seasonal event. These nobles put maples on their palms and composed poems on the beauty of the colors. The Japanese people sense the beginning of autumn when small Japanese maple leaves turn red.

Momiji Manju, a specialty in Hiroshima, are maple shaped red bean cake.

November

November 15th is a festival for boys for three and five years old, girls for three and seven years old. The festival is called *Shichi-Go-San*, "Seven-Five-Three." The purpose of this celebration is for parents to wish their children to grow up healthy. Children of these years wear kimonos and go to a shrine to pray for their bright future.

This custom started in November 15, 1681 (in the lunar calendar) to pray for the healthy growth of the fifth Shogun's first son. Soon after, this custom spread to the common people throughout Japan.

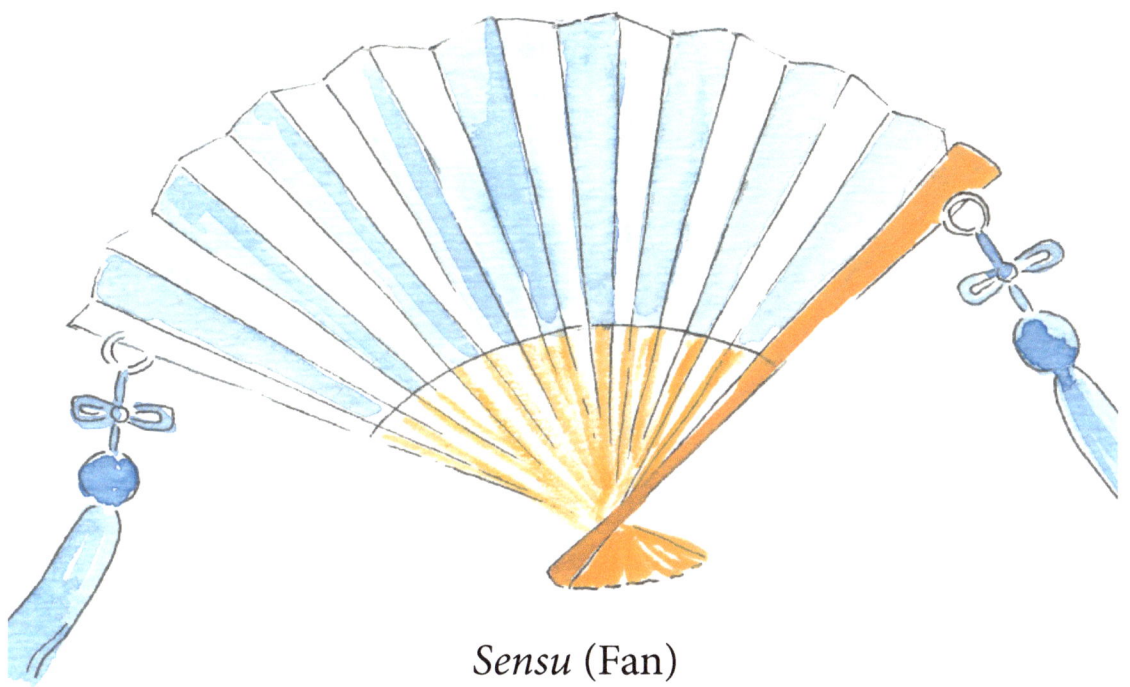

Sensu (Fan)

These children are offered pink and white long stick candies called *Chitose-ame* by their parents. They are about 7 inches long and a half inch in diameter. *Chitose* means a thousand years. These candies convey the parents' wish that their children will live long. Usually, these candies are in rectangular paper bags with printed cranes and tortoises, symbolizing long life and auspiciousness.

On the day of *Shichi-Go-San*, families with three year old girls or boys, five year old boys or seven year old girls have a busy day. Children need to wear kimonos, put on make up, pose for pictures, and go to a shrine. For children, this is a very exhausting and uncomfortable day.

Kanzashi,
(Hair accessory)

December

December 31 is the day to prepare for the New Year. Most Japanese families clean their houses thoroughly to welcome the New Year God on January First. Some families pound steamed rice into sticky rice cake to offer to God. At night, most Japanese people eat *soba*, buckwheat noodles. Japanese people wish to live as long as the noodles.

People ring the bells at temples for a total of 108 times to purify human minds of worldly desires. In Buddhism, these desires are causes of both physical and mental troubles. Therefore, it is important for Buddhists to clean their minds entirely.

Before people ring the bell, they have to fold their hands in prayer in front of the bells. They ring the bell 107 times on New Year's Eve, and one time on New Year's Day. For the Japanese people, December 31 is the day to cleanse their houses and souls in order to have a bright new year.

Toshikoshi Soba,
(New Year's Eve Noodles)

Ari Idee was born in Japan in 1976.
She graduated with a B.A. in Art from
Ueno Gakuen University in 1999 and
a B.A in English Literature from
Meiji Gakuin University in 2003.

http://aribooks.com